# Finding Out About

## Seaside Holidays

*Ian Bild and Stephen Humphries*

Batsford Academic and Educational Ltd, London

# Contents

| | |
|---|---|
| Introduction | 3 |
| Useful Sources | 4 |
| Book List | 4 |
| Taking the Seawater | 6 |
| Royalty and the Seaside in the Late Eighteenth Century | 8 |
| Getting Away in Early Victorian Times | 10 |
| Crowded Beaches in the Late Nineteenth Century | 12 |
| The Twentieth Century | 14 |
| Where People Stayed | 16 |
| Working in a Seaside Town | 18 |
| Bathing Machines and Dippers | 20 |
| Swimming Costumes and Nude Bathing | 22 |
| The Sea | 24 |
| Seaside Memories | 26 |
| Piers | 28 |
| Pier Mishaps | 30 |
| Seaside Fun and Entertainments | 32 |
| Pierrot Players and Punch and Judy | 34 |
| Rescue at Sea | 36 |
| Rich and Poor Holidays | 38 |
| Holiday Camps | 40 |
| Seaside Postcards | 42 |
| Holidays Today | 44 |
| Difficult Words | 46 |
| Biographical Notes | 46 |
| Map | 47 |
| Index | 48 |

*The picture on the title page shows a Punch and Judy Show, Ilfracombe, 1894.*

© Ian Bild and Stephen Humphries, 1983
First published 1983

All rights reserved. No part of this publication may be reproduced, in any form or by any means, without permission from the Publisher

Typeset by Tek-Art Ltd, London SE20
and printed in Great Britain by
R.J. Acford Ltd
Chichester, Sussex
for the publishers
Batsford Academic and Educational Ltd,
an imprint of B T Batsford Ltd,
4 Fitzhardinge Street,
London W1H 0AH

ISBN 0 7134 4439 8

## ACKNOWLEDGMENTS

The authors and publishers would like to thank the following for their kind permission to reproduce copyright illustrations: Aerofilms Ltd, page 17; Janice Anderson, page 23 (bottom); Bristol Omnibus Co Ltd, page 15; BBC Hulton Picture Library, pages 7, 12 (top); British Railways, page 11; L.W. Cozens, page 31; The Herne Bay Records Society, page 28; Pat Hodgson Library, page 23 (top); Marjorie Humphries, page 27; The Illustrated London News Picture Library, page 12 (bottom); The Kodak Museum, page 38; Lancashire County Council, page 9 (bottom); Manchester Public Libraries, page 10; Royal National Lifeboat Institution, page 37; Dave Saunders, page 45; Sefton Libraries and Arts Services, page 29; South Avon Mercury, page 31; South Eastern Newspapers Ltd, page 30; Victoria and Albert Museum, frontispiece; Weymouth and Portland Borough Council, page 9 (top). The map on page 47 was drawn by Rudolph Britto.

The extracts on pages 18 and 19 are from Winstanley, *Life in Kent* (William Dawson and Sons Ltd); on page 14 from Delgado, *The Annual Outing and Other Excursions* (George Allen & Unwin); and on pages 38-39 from Thea Thompson, *Edwardian Childhoods* (Routledge & Kegan Paul Ltd).

# Introduction

Most of us have been to the seaside at sometime or other in our lives. We go for various reasons — to get away from it all, to rest, sunbathe, rush around, dig holes in the sand, swim... generally, to have a good time.

Have people always gone to the seaside? Have they always gone for the same reasons? Have they always done the same sorts of things? How has the seaside holiday changed over the years?

We will try to answer these and other questions in this book. Each section dips into a particular topic — sunbathing, holiday camps, entertainment, rescue at sea and many others. The idea is then for you, using the extracts as a starting point, to find out more about the particular subjects that you find interesting.

We will discover that the seaside holiday is relatively new. It all began around the beginning of the eighteenth century. Some wealthy people of the day decided that they could cure many of their illnesses by going off to places like Scarborough or Weymouth and dipping themselves in the sea.

George III and George IV themselves developed a passion for the seaside, and the idea took off. Tiny fishing villages suddenly grew into fashionable seaside resorts for wealthy people. Opulent buildings sprang up everywhere.

It was not until the middle of the nineteenth century that the seaside holiday became more popular and available to working-class people. With the Industrial Revolution, increased population in the towns and the development of railways, the day trip to the sea was something that many people could and wanted to do.

Cities were — and still can be — grim places in which to live, and the excursion to the seaside offered an exciting escape from the pollution and toil, to the pleasures of fresh air, relaxation and fun.

Of course, week-long holidays were unheard-of for most people, until quite recently. It was not till the Second World War that paid holidays became normal. They were fought for for fifty years, mainly by people involved in trade unions.

The seaside holiday has seen some interesting changes over the years. For instance, sunbathing only became popular in the 1920s. Before that, people were more concerned about keeping a pale complexion. They used creams to stop themselves getting brown, and women used parasols to protect themselves from the sun.

Bathing habits have also changed. Well into the nineteenth century, people went into the sea naked or wearing flimsy costumes. Once Victorian attitudes got a firmer hold on society, this all changed and people were anxious to cover themselves up; men were

*A tranquil but crowded scene on a beach at Brighton in the 1940s. What else did people do at the seaside, apart from lying on the beach?*

## Useful Sources

segregated from the women on the beaches. In the twentieth century we are coming back to flimsy costumes and nude bathing — in some places.

More recently, we have seen the rise of the Holiday Camp and many people going abroad. The car, the aeroplane and increased incomes have once again changed the nature of the seaside holiday.

Most of us now go on holiday — many of us to the seaside. It is important to think that, every time we go on holiday, we are actually making history.

### Book List

Many books for adults, about seaside holidays, contain excellent illustrations and are well worth referring to, in your local library. Books listed here with a * were published some while ago, but you may also find them in your library.

Adamson, Simon, *Seaside Piers*, Batsford, 1977
Anderson, J. and Swinglehurst, E., *The Victorian and Edwardian Seaside*, Hamlyn
*Barton, M. and Sitwell, O., *Brighton*, 1935
*Cloud, Yvonne, *Beside the Seaside*, 1934
*Clunn, Harold, *Famous South Coast Pleasure Resorts Past and Present*, 1929
Delgado, A., *The Annual Outing and Other Excursions*, Allen & Unwin, 1977
*Eyre, Kathleen, *Bygone Blackpool*
*Harper, C.G., *The Kentish Coast*, 1914
Holt, T.V., *Postcards of the Golden Age,* London, 1971
Lindley, Kenneth, *Seaside Architecture*, Evelyn, 1973
*Mate, C. and Riddle, C., *Bournemouth 1810-1910*, 1910
*Moorhouse, Sydney, *Holiday Lancashire*
Pimlott, J., *The Englishman's Holiday*, Harvester, 1947 and 1976
*Reynolds, Harry, *Minstrel Memories*
Steers, J.A., *The Coast of England and Wales in Pictures*, Cambridge University Press, 1978
Walvin, J., *Beside the Seaside*, Allen Lane, 1978
*Wanklyn, C., *Lyme Regis, a Retrospect*, 1922

### 1. LIVING MEMORY

Your own experiences can be a very useful starting point. What do you remember about your own holidays? What did you do? Where did you stay? Ask yourselves these questions and you might be surprised at the amount of detailed information that comes out. Then ask your parents and grandparents about their experiences. You might want to ask friends, other relatives or neighbours about their seaside holidays. There may be old people living in your street who are only too glad to talk to you. You can begin to build up a very interesting picture of the way the seaside holiday has changed — or not — within living memory.

If you can get hold of a cassette tape recorder, then do so. You will find it very useful indeed. Before you go round interviewing people, make sure you know how your tape-recorder works. Practise on yourself. Also make sure that the machine is in good working order, and see how close to the microphone someone has to be, for a good recording.

It is also useful to prepare a list of questions to ask: When did you first go to the seaside? What were your first impressions? How long did you stay for? How did you get there? Did anything funny happen while you were there? The questions that you could ask are endless. Choose perhaps a dozen.

You do not have to stick rigidly to the questions you have prepared. They should be used as a guide or a prompt if there is a lull in the conversation. With some people you cannot get a word in edgeways. Don't worry! Sometimes it is better not to break the flow.

When you have finished your recordings, listen to them, choose the pieces that are of interest to you and write or type them out. This can be a long, slow job. It is called transcribing. The material that you have produced can then be read by other people.

History goes back beyond living memory and, of course, things happen in our own lifetimes which we cannot directly experience. So we have also to turn to other sources of information to help us build up a more complete picture.

2. BOOKS, GENERAL
The Book List gives a list of published books that should be available in most main libraries. One in particular — *The Englishman's Holiday* by J. Pimlott — gives a very detailed bibliography, which you might find useful.

3. BOOKS, LOCAL
You will probably be interested in one or two resorts in particular. The main library or reference library in the chosen resort is usually the best place to go. Explain to the librarian what sort of books you are looking for and he or she will show you how to go about finding them in their card indexes.

4. LOCAL GUIDES
Local guides, maps and timetables, both recent and old ones, can be a mine of information. Some reference libraries have a wide range of guides from all over the country. Otherwise, if possible, you will have to go to the reference library of your chosen resort.

5. NOVELS, LETTERS, MEMOIRS
Many writers have written about the seaside as part of larger works. You might remember something you have read by Dickens or Laurie Lee. If you think something in this area might be useful for you, use your initiative and ask your English or history teacher or the local librarian.

6. SURVEYS AND REPORTS
Official reports such as the Census can be useful for studying the growth of a particular resort. Surveys such as Charles Booth's *Life and Labour of the People in London* (1889-1902) can also be helpful.

7. NEWSPAPERS AND PERIODICALS
If you are studying a particular resort you will find newspapers and periodicals from the town particularly useful. These are kept in the main reference library in the town. Adverts about holidays in the local and national press are also revealing.

8. PHOTOGRAPHS AND ILLUSTRATIONS
Many interesting pictures have been published in the books mentioned in the Book List. Often the library, records office or local museum will have large photograph collections.

9. POSTCARDS
Postcards can be very informative. Recent postcards are readily available at shops and kiosks, and you probably already have some that have been sent to you. Old postcards can be found in reference libraries or sometimes in shops that specialize in old stamps and cards, or on stalls in local markets.

HOW TO GO ABOUT GETTING INFORMATION
We have mentioned reference libraries. The local archives or records office can also be valuable, as can local museums.

Sometimes, information is difficult to come by. A letter to a local newspaper or radio station, asking for people to come forward with memories and information, can be very fruitful. But, more likely, you will find yourselves with too much material. In this case, you need to decide what is important and what is not and to try to organize your material as simply and as effectively as possible.

# Taking the Seawater

The first seaside holiday-makers were wealthy people. The craze only started in the early eighteenth century and till the nineteenth century people did not go to sunbathe, swim or dig holes in the sand. They went to drink or immerse themselves in the water. They believed that seawater was a cure for practically every illness. The privileged minority were the only people with the time and money to spend at the seaside — which could offer more than the limited inland spas.

In 1752, Richard Russel, a fashionable "quack", wrote his *Dissertation on the Use of Seawater*. Amongst other things, he believed that seawater was good for constipation and he would order his patients — all of them rich — to go and drink the water at Southampton or Brighthelmstone. Here are two extracts from his book.

### A "COMMON DEFENCE"

That vaſt Collection of Waters which we call the Sea, *ſurrounds the whole Earth, and conſequently waſhes whatever is contained between its oppoſite Shores, as Submarine Plants, Salts, Fiſhes, Minerals etc and is therefore enrich'd with the Particles it receives from theſe Bodies .... All theſe Cauſes ſeem jointly to conſtitute this Fluid which we call the Sea and which the omniſcient Creator of all Things, ſeems to have defign'd to be a Kind of common Defence againſt the Corruption and Putrefaction of Bodies ...

*In eighteenth-century English the letter "s" often becomes an "f" and nouns have capital letters.

---

A
DISSERTATION
On the USE of
SEA-WATER
IN THE
DISEASES of the GLANDS.
PARTICULARLY
The *Scurvy, Jaundice, King's-Evil, Leproſy*, and the *Glandular Conſumption*.

Tranſlated from the *Latin* of
RICHARD RUSSEL, M.D.

The THIRD EDITION, Reviſed and Corrected.

To which is added,
A COMMENTARY on SEA-WATER,
Tranſlated from the *Latin* of
J. SPEED, M.D.

Both by an EMINENT PHYSICIAN.

LONDON:
Printed for W. OWEN, at *Homer's* Head, *Temple-Bar*.
MDCCLV.

---

Why did people go to the seaside in the eighteenth century? Try to find out about other people who were "cured" by seawater.

Scarborough in the 1730s was one of the very first ▷ "watering places". A certain Dr Wittie said that the water of Scarborough "cleanses the stomach, opens the lungs, cures Asthma and Scurvey, purifies the blood ... and [is] a most sovereign Remedy against Hypochondrik Melancholly and Windiness". Here you can see the horses pulling the bathing machines into the water.

## ST VITUS'S DANCE

There is alfo another Cafe that is worthy of Notice, in which I lately experienced Sea-Water to be extreamly benificial. A youth of Sixteen, a Scholar of Winchefter School.... About the Middle of September 1748, his School-fellows obferv'd him making ftrange Motions with his Hands and Arms, and his Eyes ftaring and diftorted, his head lying fometimes upon one Shoulder and fometimes on the other while speaking; and other ridiculous Motions of his Limbs, fuch as Sydenham defcribes in the Difeafe called St. Vitus's Dance. In this Youth the Mufcles of the Tongue and Pharynx were so relaxed that he could fcarcely fpeak any words articulately, or fwallow any food. As he lay in Bed his Tongue came out beyond his Teeth, and the Spittle flow'd out continually.... About the Beginning of November when things grew worfe I was confulted... I advifed to send him immediately to Southampton, as well for the Convenience of drinking the Sea-Water as bathing in the Sea. Being carry'd thither he was put into the Sea the 17th of November, and afterwards every other Day...

November 24. This Night and every Day after, he drank a half a Pint of Sea-Water, either going in Bed or early in the Morning, and bath'd in the Sea every Day.

November 30. His Appetite return'd, his Limbs were ftronger, and his Words pronounced more articulately.

December 12. He came from Bathing daily brifker and ftronger and readier in expreffing his Words.... Therefore I ordered him to continue in the fame Method till he had recover'd his perfect Health...

February 8. The Patient came to Oxford, healthy and ftrong, to fee his friends, and take fome Recreation intending foon to return to Winchefter.

◁ The front cover of Richard Russel's Dissertation. Does it tell you anything about how the book sold?

# Royalty and the Seaside

In the late eighteenth century small seaside villages like Brighton, Weymouth, Margate and Bridlington suddenly blossomed into attractive seaside resorts. Improvements in transport allowed people to go further afield. The fashionable people who went to take the water in these places required fashionable facilities and so the resorts developed. Some, like Weymouth, were particularly favoured by royalty.

## GEORGE III AT WEYMOUTH

In 1789 George III "nobly" immersed himself at Weymouth. He went there because he was told it was a quiet, respectable little town. Here is a description of the town when he arrived:

> They have dressed out every street with labels, 'God Save the King'. The bathing machines make it their motto over all their windows, and those bathers that belong to the royal dippers wear it in bandeaus on their bonnets to go into the sea; and have it again in large letters round their waists, to encounter the waves. Think of the surprise of his Majesty when, the first time of his bathing, he had no sooner popped his royal head under the water than a band of music concealed in a neighbouring machine struck up, God Save Great George Our King.

This extract is from the Diary of Fanny Burney, Second Keeper of the Robes to Queen Charlotte and a member of the Weymouth holiday parties. Compare it with the humorous drawing of the "Royal Dipping".

*George III's first bathe at Weymouth, 1789. He is being helped by a dipper, or bathing woman, whose job it was to hold on to people while they "took the water". The bathing machines on wheels in the background were pulled into the sea, often by horses, providing a platform and some privacy for the bathers.*

## BLACKPOOL ON OFFER

Blackpool in the 1790s was visited not only by the Lancashire gentry but also by "rich, rough, honest manufacturers". Here, George Cook, a local hotelier, advertised in the Manchester papers what he had to offer to potential customers:

> **Gunpowder, Hyson, Souchong and Congou teas of the first quality; White's Cocoa, coffee, chocolate, loaf and brown sugar, sago, tapioca, spices of all kinds and other groceries; Jewellry of the newest fashion from one of the first houses in London. An assortment of hosiery, millinery, linen, drapery ... bathing caps and dresses ... The public room will be furnished with a library of books, a large collection of copper plate engravings ... newspapers and magazines etc.; and in the billiard room is a handsome table and everything necessary to render that genteel amusement agreeable to the company. Ladies may have anything made in the genteelest manner and at the shortest notice.**

How were people expected to spend their time on holiday? Did they go bathing, as in Weymouth?

*Try to find pictures of present-day Blackpool and compare them with this illustration. Are any of the 1784 landmarks still standing?*

# in the Late Eighteenth Century

Royal Dipping.

BLACKPOOL IN 1784.

A Spring Well.
B Mrs Baileys Bathing House.
C Arching Ground.
D Bowling Green.
E Mr Baileys Tavern.
F Alcove.
G Mr Forshaw's Tavern.
H Mr Crookes & Post Office
I Mrs Hudsons Tavern.
K Mr Hulls Tavern.
L Nr Boneys Wine House.
M Nr Elsons.
N Ancient Roman Building.
O Public Walks.

# Getting Away

Many coastal hamlets and fishing villages grew rapidly into seaside towns in early Victorian times. As the Industrial Revolution developed and the population of the towns grew, so the need to get away from the grim surroundings increased. The seaside offered a complete change for people and, with the growth of the railways and cheap transport, the possibilities of getting away improved. Some workplaces began to allow official holidays — usually a day here or there. Some organized the first excursions, and many workers took "unauthorised" time off. Margate, Eastbourne, Southend, Worthing, Blackpool — amongst other places — became popular.

◁ *Railway advertisement from the 1840s for excursions to the sea from the Lancashire towns. How long did it take to get from Manchester to Fleetwood? In those days women paid less than men.*

### EXCURSION TO HASTINGS

Here is a non-too-complimentary description of some Londoners on an excursion trip to Hastings in 1857, taken from the *Illustrated Times*:

> [They] swarm upon the beach, wandering listlessly about with apparently no other aim than to get a mouthful of fresh air. You may see them in groups of three or four: the husband—a pale, overwrought man, dressed in black frock-coat, figured waistcoat and bright blue tie—carried the baby; the wife, equally pale and thin, decked out in her best, labours after with a basket of "prog". And then there is generally another child, one remove above the baby, wandering aimlessly behind. She must bear the burden until church-time is

# in Early Victorian Times

## DESECRATION OF THE SABBATH

Some clergymen were appalled that railway excursions to the seaside kept people away from church on Sundays and were a "desecration of the Sabbath". Here, the Archdeacon of St Mary's, Southampton, Joseph Wigram, quotes in 1853 the experiences of a "Christian Observer" who reported that:

> Thousands, and tens of thousands have been led, during the summer season, to travel by the South Western Railway on the Lord's-day, causing to an awful extent the desecration of the Sabbath, even to such an extent, that the Railway Servants have been kept in a complete state of Sabbath Slavery, bound down to incessant labour. It may truly be said of many of them, that they know not a day of rest. That which is a day of rest and freedom to others, is a day of labour and slavery to them. The very freedom others enjoy, is the cause of their slavery, for during the Sunday, on the South-Western Railway, there are many more travelling than on any other day of the week. I have myself witnessed the awful scene of Sabbath Desecration at the Waterloo Terminus, between the hours of eight and ten in the morning, from three to six o'clock in the afternoon, and from ten to eleven at night.

over; and the public houses will be open, a quart of porter in the pewter will be forthcoming and the family will dine *alfresco* on the beach.

"Prog" was the food for the day out. How were the family dressed?

Try to find out more about why people went to the seaside in the 1840s and 1850s. Why did clergymen disapprove?

*This music cover shows people jam-packed in the third-class compartment on their way to the seaside. Note the contrast with the first-class compartment a little further down the train. (1862)*

# Crowded Beaches

With paid holidays becoming more regular, and the railway and road networks more fully established, the seaside holiday became very popular by the end of the nineteenth century. The beaches were now crowded and more facilities and grander entertainments were provided to keep people occupied and to take their money. Still, the day excursion was all that most people could afford — at weekends or on Bank Holidays, which were introduced in 1871. Only the middle classes could afford to go away for longer.

A children's trip to Bognor in 1913. The buckets and spades are the same as today, but the styles of dress are very different.

Waiting for the excursion train, 1880. Note the different styles of dress on show on the platform. The picture captures the bustle of the day out to the seaside, though some of the people look remarkably calm.

## in the Late Nineteenth Century

### THE JOYS OF THE SEASIDE

Here is part of a song written in 1888, called *The Joys of the Seaside*. It describes very vividly a typical seaside town, and what you did there.

Then what j'y to go a-bything—though
   you'll swim, if you're a sly thing,
Like a mermaid nimbly writhing, with a
   foot upon the sand!
When you're tired of old Poseidon, there's
   the pier to promenade on,
Strauss, and Sullivan, and Haydn form the
   programme of the band.

        Chorus
For there's always a band at the Sea-side!
If I'd only my w'y I would de-cide
   To dwell evermore,
   By the murmuring shore,
With the billows a-blustering be-side!

And, with boatmen so beguiling, sev'ral
   parties go out siling!
Sitting all together smiling, handing
   sandwiches about,
To the sound of concertiner—till they're
   gradually greener,
And they wish the ham was leaner, as
   they sip their bottled stout.

        Chorus
And they cry, 'Put us back on the
   Sea-side! etc.'

There is pleasure unalloyed in hiring hacks
   and going roiding!
(If you stick on tight, avoiding any
   cropper or mishap),
Or about the rocks you ramble; over
   boulders slip and scramble;
Or sit down and do a gamble, playing
   'Loo' or 'Penny Nap'.

        Chorus
'Penny Nap' is the gyme for the Sea-side!
   etc.

Then it's lovely to be spewning, all the
   glamour of the mewn in,
With your love his banjo tewning, ere
   flirtation can begin!
As along the sands you're strowling, till
   the hour of ten is towling,
And your Ma, severely scowling, asks
   'Wherever have you bin?'

        Chorus
Then you answer, 'I've been by the
   Sea-side! etc.'

Should the sky be dark and frowning, and
   the restless wind be mowning,
With the breakers' thunder drowning all
   the laughter and the glee;
And the day should prove a drencher out
   of doors you will not ventcher,
But you'll read the volumes lent yer by
   the Local Libraree!

        Chorus
For there's sure to be one at the Sea-side!
   etc.

What does the song tell you about the seaside holiday at the end of the last century? Try to find out the different places that people went to at that time.

13

# The Twentieth Century

This century has seen the growth in size of the seaside resorts. Paid holidays have become longer, incomes have increased and so more people are able to go away. The car has made a great difference, giving people added mobility. But has the seaside holiday itself changed? Some holidays have become much more organized — for example, holiday camps and tours; some entertainments have developed on a grander scale — amusement arcades, fun fairs. But there is still the sea, the sun, the beach, the donkeys, Punch and Judy . . . .

## CATCHING THE TRAIN TO THE SEA, 1936

Day outings have remained very popular to the present day. For poorer people and children, they were still the only way of getting to the seaside. Not everybody could afford to go for longer.

In this extract Mr A.J. Taylor recalls a day trip to Hunstanton in 1936, by train:

> The sun always seemed to shine on that crowded platform. It smelled of shell-fish, newsprint, disinfectant—and the lime-encrusted urinal at the far end. It was too late in the year for daffodils and tulips but there were a few cardboard boxes of cut flowers stacked on a trolley waiting for the Peterborough train. And a few early punnets of strawberries. There was a marvellous happy sort of chaos—trippings over push-chairs, buckets and spades; a faded last-year's Union Jack, baskets and string bags holding sandwiches and the towels and costumes for bathing and paddling . . . .
>
> For their day out the males old enough to wear long trousers would display white shirts, braces, and freshly-whitened plimsolls—or brown sandals with perforated uppers and crêpe soles. As the time approached the late arrivals would join the jostling to get a good seat. Families manœuvred and mothers shepherded in the hope of cornering a compartment to themselves.
>
> The train would be too long for the platform; as it approached there would be frantic snatchings and shrieks . . . When one half of the train had been filled to bursting point it would "draw up" . . . . The rear end would get into Hunstanton first—a precious six-coach lengths nearer the ticket barrier . . .
>
> Outside the station we poured on to the Green—elegant sloping lawns in front of the Sandringham Hotel . . . Deck chairs for adults, raincoats for children if the sand was damp. The first paddle, then bathing costumes on and really into the sea if the water was warm enough. Grandmas tucked dresses in to knicker legs and displayed varicose veins and massive, blotchy, bleached thighs . . .
>
> Then we had boiled ham sandwiches, bottle of lemon barley or yellow lemonade made from two ounces of crystals bought from the corner-shop. We made mammoth sand-castles; there were long walks to the water's edge for buckets which spilled half their contents on the way back.
>
> The final ritual would be a visit to the shops in the town, where Mums marvelled at the very high seaside prices . . . Getting to the station early was surely an adult ploy, and we were never first.

What did people take with them to the seaside?

## BRIGHTON, 1960s

This piece appeared in *Holiday Haunts*, 1966, and gives a factual description of what was available to the holiday-maker in Brighton:

> An all-the-year round resort, Brighton has everything for the holidaymaker. Beach, sand and shingle, shelves gently. Six miles of front, beautiful scenery, a dry and bracing climate, and abundant entertainment. Two piers (Palace and West), indoor and outdoor swimming pools, five golf courses, aquarium, race track, greyhound racing, county cricket (at Hove), league football, tennis, bowls, boating, sea and freshwater fishing, water skiing, camping and caravan sites. Children's bathing and paddling pools and playgrounds, three theatres (many plays are seen there before going to London), twelve cinemas, three ballrooms, ice shows, sports arena, variety shows. Leading orchestras play at the Dome. The Royal Pavilion, built for the Prince Regent (later George IV) is open to the public. Exhibits include some on loan from Buckingham Palace. The ancient Lanes are world famous for their antique shops. The Downs with their peaceful villages add to the appeal of this part of the South coast.

Compare the two extracts. What do they tell you about the changes that have taken place between the 1930s and 1960s? Find out from your parents and grandparents what they think the main changes have been.

*The Bedminster Ebenezer Sisterhood outing (a Methodist Church outing), on 27 June 1922, in charabancs on hire from the Bristol Bus Company. The driver sits towards the middle and he is flanked by passengers on either side. Can you spot the number of people in each charabanc?*

# Where People Stayed

The wealthy people who first went to the seaside stayed in large and ornate hotels; but, as the less well-off took the opportunity of staying for any length of time, so an array of different types of accommodation sprung up: first, smaller hotels, then boarding houses and later bed and breakfast, caravans, chalets and tents. Look around any large seaside town today and you should find this whole range of accommodation.

*A letter from the manager of a private hotel in Eastbourne. Why do you think "light" is mentioned?*

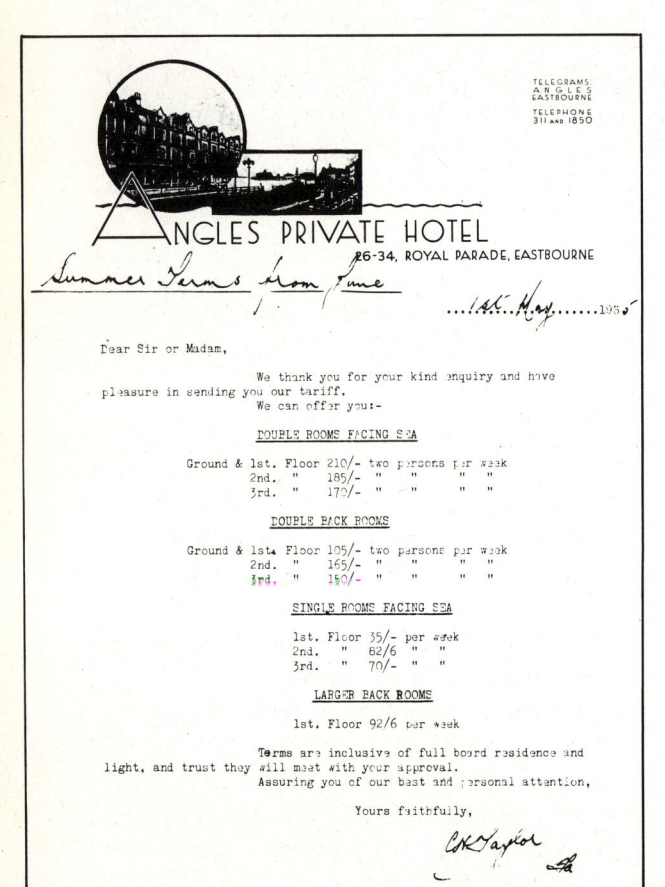

## STAYING IN A GUEST HOUSE, 1920s–'30s

Jim Humphries was born in 1921 at Stoke on Trent, the son of a miner. He remembers staying in a guest house in the late 1920s and '30s:

> We often used to go to Southport for our holidays. It used to only be for three or four days; go Saturday and come back Tuesday, because we couldn't afford any more. We stayed at a guest house, all of us in the same room, a family room. It was common then to buy your own food and the owner would cook it for you. There would be things like bacon for breakfast and meat and veg. for dinner. In those days you reckoned to put weight on when you went on holiday. You'd weigh yourself before you went and weigh yourself when you came back. That was true of children especially. It wasn't like it is today with people wanting to lose weight all the time. You wanted to put some on, on holiday, to last you through the year, through the hard times.

## CARAVANS AND CHALETS

In this extract, Hedley Bashforth, who is now a teacher, remembers staying in a caravan and a chalet during the 1950s:

> I always thought Mablethorpe was a funny name for a seaside place. At first I thought it must be something to do with my Grandmam whose name was Mabel. But she always went to Blackpool.
> We used to stay in one of the hundreds of caravans berthed all along the open

*A sprawling caravan site in Porthcawl. What do you think are the advantages and disadvantages of a caravan holiday?*

Why do you think people wanted to put on weight when on holiday in the 1930s? Compare and contrast a holiday in a guest house with one in a chalet or caravan.

grass next to the miles of dunes. The centre of activity for the beach was the refreshment hut which served up thousands of jugs of tea every day. I got locked in to the lavatory and it took Mum and Dad half an hour to get me out. I thought I was going to have to spend the week in there.

Sometimes we went up the coast to Humberstone to collect a couple of buckets full of cockles. We shelled them and soaked them in vinegar.

One year we stayed in a chalet in the holiday village at Trusthorpe, which is next to Mablethorpe. This was a great luxury, and there was plenty of room for the seven of us who stayed.

On the way back home from Mablethorpe in our Lanchester (1936) we always used to stop at the same farm shop near Louth to get bread and eggs. I never smelt bread like that anywhere else.

# Working in a Seaside Town

While we are enjoying ourselves on holiday, other people who live and work at the seaside work long and hard, and are often poorly paid; particularly the seasonal workers who are employed during the busiest periods. Try to compile a list of the people you might find working at the seaside today.

## HELPING IN A GUEST HOUSE

Florence Parker was born in 1896. Until she was married she lived with her grandmother who was a landlady at Margate, and she spent much of her childhood helping her:

> There were four bedrooms and then a big attic which my aunt, nan and I had to share. Then we had a basement kitchen but that was all shut off in the winter. We had all the comfort in the winter and we always had the best rooms then.
>
> Sometimes you had to do cooking and attendance. They'd bring their own food in and you'd cook it and dish it all up. Then you only charged them so much a week for the room. If you got twenty-five bob a week you were lucky. If you'd got an extra big family perhaps you would work thirty bob a week out of it. If you did bed and breakfast they wouldn't pay you more than a couple of bob a night.
>
> It was blinkin' hard work. Daily routine would be up in the morning, they'd all want cups of tea.... you'd have to get their tray ready and if they went out before breakfast you'd to go up there, empty the slops, make the bed and lay the breakfast. Then you had to cook the breakfast and have that ready by the time they came in. You'd have to do that to all the rooms, see. Then you had to wait for them to go out and then go and collect all the trays. Then you had the basement to do and all those stairs. You'd go out with your brush and dust pan, broom and

◁ *A Brighton postcard from the 1900s. What aspects of the seaside town do you think are missing? Look also at the extract from* Holiday Haunts *on page 15.*

## A PAGE BOY AT THE ROYAL KENT HOTEL

Albert Packman was born in the country at Hernhill near Faversham in 1892. His ambition was to be a page boy, and he managed to get a job at the Royal Kent Hotel at Sandgate. He was paid five shillings a week.

> Five shillings a week all for myself! Nothing to buy, no food, just my clothes. I was fourteen and a half. So five shillings a week, good Lord, I was a millionaire before I started. . . .
>
> I was upstairs in a room with all the others. There was a hall porter, head waiter, waiters, cook, chamber maids, I think there was about twenty servants all told. I thought it was smashing. We'd get down there teatime in the servants' hall, the lot of us there. I'd never known anything like it. Brought up in a little tiny three house place where you never met anybody, just the school people and those from the houses down there. To go there and mix with all these people at that table! . . .
>
> As a rule they had about thirty people staying there and I had all the crockery to wash up for all these people. Three or four course, maybe more. The saucepans and all the plates and dishes. I had a double sink and big draining board and all the rest of it. The first night I thought I'm not going to wear my best clothes for washing up so I put my boots on. Anyway I got in there and I had to go up three steps from the scullery into the kitchen and I had to collect all this dirty stuff. I come out of there with all these plates up my chin, I wanted to show I could do it all right. You can just imagine it, can't you. Three steps to go down. I forgot all about them. You never heard such a clatter in all your life. I went down and the plates shot through all on the stone floor, the flagstones in the scullery. I thought, "This is it. My five bob's gone. I've lost my job and everything." The missus, it was a woman that owned it, she came running out there.
>
> "Oh," I said, "I'm awfully sorry. I really am sorry. I won't do it again. It was these boots. I shall get some lighter shoes to wear. I'll pay for them at so much a week. I won't do it again, honestly."
>
> She said, "Oh, don't worry about that, but do try and be more careful, that's all."
>
> I thought that's not so bad. I got through that.

> duster, top of the house down, each room and staircase.
>
> Cheerful sort of people we used to have in those days. Nan always had her little book. You know, who came, when they came, and what they paid. If there was somebody came and you didn't like them, you put a cross against their name. No more. You had some of them so often she used to look in her book and say, "So and so hasn't been this year. I wonder if they've died."

What differences can you see between working in a guest house and working in a hotel in the early part of the century?

# Bathing Machines and Dippers

Bathing machines were introduced in the eighteenth century. They were pulled by horses into the sea and were designed to give people a certain amount of privacy. In later years, some had canopies that could be pulled right down to the sea. For many years it was common for men and women to bathe naked or to wear thin clinging costumes. Then some Victorians thought it was immoral and dangerous for members of the opposite sex to see each other with little or no clothes on and the sexes were kept apart.

## BATHING MACHINES IN THE EIGHTEENTH CENTURY

A character in Tobias Smollett's novel, *Humphry Clinker* (1771), described the use of bathing machines in the eighteenth century. He was describing Scarborough.

> Image to yourself a small, snug, wooden chamber, fixed on a wheel-carriage, having a door at each end, and, on each side, a little window above, a bench below. . . . guides who attend the ladies in the water are of their own sex; and they and the female bathers have a dress of flannel for the sea; nay, they are provided with other conveniences for the support of decorum. A certain number of the machines are fitted with tilts, that project from the seaward ends of them, so as to screen the bathers from the view of all persons whatsoever. The beach is admirably adapted for this practice, the descent being gently gradual, and the sand soft as velvet; but then the machines can be used only at a certain time of the tide, which varies every day; so that sometimes the bathers are obliged to rise very early in the morning.
>
> For my part, I love swimming as an exercise, and can enjoy it at all times of the tide, without the formality of an apparatus.

## MARTHA GUNN

Martha Gunn was the head bathing woman at Brighton, dipping "fine" ladies in the sea in the late eighteenth century. She was originally the wife of a fisherman. She went on working as a "dipper" into extreme old age. Asked by an aristocrat how she was, she said:

> Well and hearty, thank God, sir, but rather hobbling; I don't bathe now because I aint so strong as I used t'be; so I superintend on the beach, for I'm up afore any of 'em; you may always find me and my pitcher at one exact spot, every morning by six o'clock.

When asked about her age, she said:

> Only eighty-eight sir; in fact eighty-nine come next Christmas pudding; and though I've lost me teeth, I can mumble it with as good relish and hearty appetite as anybody.
>
> While I've life and health, I must be bustling away my old friends and benefactors; I think I ought to be proud, for I've had as many bows from man, woman and child as the Prince hisself; aye, and I do believe the very dogs in the town know me.

*The bathing place at Ramsgate in 1788. Many people are taking the water with no clothes on or in flimsy gowns. The bathing machines were driven back to the beach by a horse. The large canopies on the bathing machines are there so that people do not have to be seen, but the people in this picture are bathing quite openly.*

## RULES AT MARGATE, 1862

Margate was a home of bathing machines and in May 1862 made certain regulations for bathers:

> **That a distance of not less than 60 feet shall be preserved by the Owners and Drivers of Bathing Machines between the Bathing Machines from which Females are bathing and those from which Males are bathing . . . .**
>
> That the Owner of every machine shall gratuitously provide for the use of female bathers engaging such Machines, gowns or dresses; and for the use of Male bathers engaging such machines, drawers, or such other suitable covering as will prevent indecent exposure of the person.
>
> That no boat or vessel let to hire for the purpose of sailing or rowing for pleasure shall approach from the sea within the distance of two hundred yards of any Bathing Machine in actual use, except for the purpose of saving life or other strictly necessary purpose.

What do you think was the purpose of these rules? What do you think Tobias Smollett's character would have thought of them?

*A more modern style of bathing machine in the early twentieth century. Bathing machines gave way, by and large, in the 1920s, to beach huts which could not be moved.*

# Swimming Costumes and Nude Bathing

Nude bathing was common right up until the 1870s, but as "Victorian morality" began to take a firmer grip on society, fashions started to change and people began to cover themselves up with ever different types of swimming costume.

*An advert for substantial Victorian-style bathing costumes, in the late nineteenth century.*

*1920s style.*

## THE OLD WAYS – STRIPPING OFF

The Reverend Francis Kilvert was loath to give way to the new morality. In 1874 he was on holiday on the Isle of Wight and in his diary entry for 12 June he wrote:

> One has to adopt the detestable custom of bathing in drawers. If ladies don't like to see men naked, why don't they keep away from the sight? ... Today, I had a pair of drawers given me which I could not keep on. The rough waves stripped them off and tore them down round my ankles. While thus fettered I was seized and flung down by a heavy sea which retreating suddenly left me lying naked on the sharp shingle from which I rose streaming with blood. After this I took the wretched and dangerous rag off and of course there were some ladies looking on as I came up out of the water.

The drawers "given" to Rev. Kilvert would have been those hired to him by the bathing machine attendant. This was a change from two years previously when he had written, while on holiday in Weston-Super-Mare:

> Many people were openly stripping on the sands a little further on and running down into the sea, and I would have done the same but I had brought down no towels of my own.

But the next day he wrote that he was:

> ... out early before breakfast this morning bathing from the sands. There was a delicious feeling of freedom in stripping in the open air and running down naked to the sea, where the waves were curling white with foam and the red morning sunshine glowing upon the naked limbs of the bathers.

The pictures show some of the changing varieties of costumes used for swimming. In what way did attitudes towards swimming costumes change towards the end of the nineteenth century? Find some photographs of your parents and grandparents at the seaside and describe their costumes.

*Some of us prefer not to be seen in a bathing costume. (1900s)*

### THE NEW MORALITY

By contrast, in 1910, it was laid down at Broadstairs, Kent, that:

> For the preservation of decency and order, every person above the age of ten years shall wear a suitable costume or dress from the neck to the knees.

*A family bathing in the early twentieth century. The man with arms on hips has a flimsy-looking costume. Note the bathing caps.*

23

# The Sea

The sea itself has always held a tremendous fascination. Its movement, its smells, its changing moods have always captured people's imaginations. Above all, the sea has a mysterious quality — and is certainly much written about.

## AN UNEXPECTED DANGER

In his novel, *Far From the Madding Crowd* (1874), Thomas Hardy describes the beauties of the sea, and its dangers:

At last he reached the summit, and a wide and novel prospect burst upon him .... The broad steely sea, marked only by faint lines, which had a semblance of being etched thereon to a degree not deep enough to disturb its general evenness, stretched the whole width of his front and round to the right, where, near the town and port of Budmouth, the sun bristled down upon it, and banished all colour, to substitute in its place a clear, oily polish. Nothing moved in sky, land, or sea, except a frill of milkwhite foam along the nearer angles of the shore, shreds of which licked the contiguous stones like tongues.

He descended and came to a small basin of sea enclosed by the cliffs. Troy's nature freshened within him; he thought he would rest and bathe here before going further. He undressed and plunged in ....

Unfortunately for Troy a current unknown to him existed ... which was awkward for a swimmer who might be taken unawares. Troy found himself carried to the left and then round in a sweep out to sea.

What do you think were Troy's feelings when he was carried out to sea?

## ROUSING SMELLS

In *Cider with Rosie* Laurie Lee captures the appeal of the sea and the seaside in the 1920s:

> The weather cleared as we drove into Weston, and we halted on the Promenade. 'The seaside,' they said: we gazed around us, but we saw no sign of the sea. We saw a vast blue sky and an infinity of mud stretching away to the shadows of Wales. But rousing smells of an invisible ocean astonished our land-locked nostrils: salt, and wet weeds, and fishy oozes; a sharp difference in every breath...
> ... we had never seen such openness, the blue windy world seemed to have blown quite flat, bringing the sky to the level of our eyebrows. Canvas booths flapped on the edge of the Prom, mouths crammed with shellfish and vinegar; there were rows of prim boarding-houses (each the size of our Vicarage); bathchairs, carriages, and donkeys; and stilted far out on the rippled mud a white pier like a sleeping dragon.
>
> The blue day was ours; we rattled our money and divided up into groups. 'Hey, Jake, Steve; let's go have a wet' — and the men shuffled off down a side street. 'I'm beat after that, Mrs Jones, ain't you? — there's a clean place down by the band-stand.' The old women nodded, and went seeking their comforts; the young ones to stare at the policemen.
>
> Meanwhile, we boys just picked up and ran; we had a world of mud to deal with. ... We whinnied like horses and charged up and down, every hoof-mark written behind us. If you stamped in this mud, you brought it alive, the footprint began to speak, it sucked and sighed and filled with water, became a foot cut out of the sky. I dug my fingers into a stretch of mud to see how deep it was, felt a hard flat pebble and drew it out and examined it in the palm of my hand. Suddenly, it cracked, and put out two claws; I dropped it in horror, and ran ...

What did the pebble turn out to be?

Why do you think the sea captures the imagination? How does the sea reflect your moods?

*A quiet sea at Chit Rocks, Sidmouth, 1900s. Children are shrimping and searching the seaweed for interesting "finds".*
▽

*Rough sea at Trevone, Padstow.*

# Seaside Memories

Charlie Chaplin has written in his autobiography about his recollections of the sea. He has become famous, and so we are interested in reading about his life. But "ordinary" people have also recorded their memories and these are often equally vivid. They capture our imagination because they are talking about the experiences of all of us.

## CHARLIE CHAPLIN AT THE SEA

In this extract from his autobiography, Charlie Chaplin gives an account of his first impressions of the sea in the 1890s, and shows how things changed over the years:

My first sight of the sea was hypnotic. As I approached it in bright sunlight from a hilly street, it looked suspended, a live quivering monster about to fall on me. The three of us took off our shoes and paddled. The tepid sea unfurling over my insteps and around my ankles and the soft yielding sand under my feet were a revelation of delight.

What a day that was—the saffron beach, with its pink and blue pails and wooden spades, its coloured tents and umbrellas, and sailing boats hurtling gaily over laughing little waves, and up on the beach other boats resting idly on their sides, smelling of seaweed and tar—the memory of it still lingers with enchantment.

In 1957 I went back to Southend and looked in vain for the narrow, hilly street from which I had seen the sea for the first time, but there were no traces of it. At the end of the town were the remnants of what seemed a familiar fishing village with old-fashioned shop-fronts. This had vague whisperings of the past—perhaps it was the odour of seaweed and tar.

## A TRIP TO EXMOUTH

Here, in a taped interview, Marjorie Humphries recalls a trip she made to Exmouth, as a child in the 1930s:

When I was a girl, we couldn't afford holidays. So the only proper holiday I ever had was when my Aunty Elsie, she lived in Exeter, would take me down to Exmouth for a week at the seaside. I can always remember the first time I walked on the wet sand in bare feet. The tide had just gone out, and my feet started to sink into the soft oozey sand. Oh it was lovely. Everything looked so huge, with the waves rushing in, and I was a little bit frightened to go into the water above my ankles. What Aunty Elsie did to get me in, she used to sit me on her back, one leg over each side. I must have looked a funny old sight with my borrowed swimming costume that was about ten sizes too big for me.

And I can remember we used to get an old treacle tin and a stick, and go looking for cockles. You could always tell where they were, because they left a trail, like a worm's trail, on the sand. Find them, dig them up with the stick, then pop them in the tin. After that we'd go crabbing in the rockpools. If we were lucky we'd hook a crab into our tin and go back for a feast, back to the little old chalet where we stayed. It was just a wooden shack really, bare floorboards with hardly a stick of furniture in it. Not like the luxury chalets you get today.

　　Aunty Elsie had a huge saucepan, and she'd get the water boiling, then put the cockles in. And you could hear them crying and screaming in the boiling water just for a few seconds before they were dead, because they were living creatures inside the shells you see. Then, pull them out with a pin and eat them with vinegar, salt, pepper, and some bread and butter. If we had a crab as well, well that was a real treat, we'd perhaps have a little bit of salad with it. That was my first taste of sea food. You couldn't afford to buy it, and anyway it was more fun to catch it and cook it for yourself.

　　They were super holidays. We'd have donkey rides, go rowing in a boat, collect seaweed, do all sorts of things. I remember I used to enjoy myself so much that I didn't want to go home. I was always sorry to leave the seaside.

Describe your first impressions of the sea. How do they compare with those of Marjorie Humphries and Charlie Chaplin?

◁ *Marjorie Humphries with Aunty Elsie. What do you notice about the clothing?*

27

# Piers

The first piers were built as landing places for passengers and goods, but by the 1830s, they began to be used as promenades and places of entertainment — for example, at Margate, Southend and Brighton. By the middle of the nineteenth century piers were built mainly for pleasure and, with their pavilions, they provided many different forms of live entertainment.

## THE BOURNEMOUTH PIER

Guide books are a useful source of information about seaside resorts. Bright's Guide to Bournemouth of 1897 gave the following description of the pier, which was used then both for entertainment and as a landing stage.

> The Pier offers an excellent promenade and resting place for those who, while wishing to enjoy the sea air, do not care to run the risk of an attack of mal de mer. Those who have no fear of this unenjoyable state flock to the landing stages, whence the splendid steamers of the Bournemouth, Swanage and Weymouth, and Bournemouth and South Coast Steam Packets, Limited, all through the summer season, take hundreds of visitors to spend a few hours at one or other of the Watering Places on our Coast between Brighton or Torquay, or run shorter trips, at intervals during the day, for those who wish to explore the beauties of Swanage, Lulworth, Alum Bay, &C.
>
> During the early hours of the morning numbers of bathers are attracted to the Pier, from the end of which they are enabled to enjoy the luxury of a dive into clear, deep water, from the springboard which is fastened at the landing stage; while in the evening, those who love to see the mantle of the night as it gradually clothes the earth can here watch the last rays of the sun behind the Dorsetshire hills, and catch a final glimpse at the twilight bay before returning to their homes.

◁ *Herne Bay Pier in 1841. It was built for seaborne visitors. In the 1870s it was replaced by a smaller pleasure pier.*

How did the use of piers change? What entertainments might you have found on a pier at the start of this century and who did they cater for? Ask your grandparents if they remember visiting a pier. Describe their experiences.

## ENTERTAINMENTS ON HASTINGS PIER

In August 1911 visitors to Hastings were offered the following entertainments, according to public notices that appeared in a local newspaper:

The pier gave rise to many different forms of entertainment. At the pierhead, Southport, "Professor Osborne" would entertain the crowds by diving into the sea either from the pier mast or from the roof of the tea-house.

---

HASTINGS PIER
*General Manager—Mr Walter Maxwell*
TODAY (THURSDAY) AUGUST 10th. Three Nights at 7.45 and Matinee Saturday at 2.25. The Great Comedian (*from Drury Lane and Daly's Theatres*)

GEORGE GRAVES
in
"KOFFO OF BOND STREET"
*Supported by full Company of London Artistes*

\* \* \*

SUNDAY AUGUST 13th. Morning at 11.30. Evening at 8.
MILITARY BAND. 8.45 ANIMATED PICTURES. All seats 2d.

\* \* \*

MONDAY AUGUST 14th. Three nights at 7.45 and Matinee Wednesday at 2.25. Mr CHAS. KENYON and London Company in
"THE PRISONER OF ZENDA"

NOTE:
Prices of Admission to the Pavilion. Orchestra Stalls (Numbered and Reserved), 2s. 6d; Stalls (Numbered and Reserved), 1s. 6d; Centre Seats, 1s; Back Centre and Side Seats, 6d; Balcony (Smoking allowed), 1s. (may be booked at 1s. 6d.)

\* \* \*

DANCING in the Shore Pavilion every Evening at 8 p.m. Admission 6d.

\* \* \*

ANIMATED PICTURES. Morning at 11.15, Afternoon at 3.15 (When Pavilion is not otherwise engaged).
Every Evening outside at 8.30

\* \* \*

GARFIELD BARRATT'S CONCERT PARTY daily at 11.15, 3.15, 7 and 8.15

\* \* \*

BATHING from Pier Landing Stage every day from 6 a.m. to 1 p.m.
High Diving; Crystal Tank Performances.
Box Ball Alleys. Shooting Saloon. Joy Wheel.
Photo Groups. Afternoon Teas, etc.

\* \* \*

# Pier Mishaps

Piers have often suffered mishaps and accidents. Jutting out into the sea, they are exposed to wind and weather and many have been destroyed by fire and other misfortunes. During the Second World War they were used as landing stages and were subject to the additional hazards of bombs and mines. A number of piers, such as Clevedon, have now been closed because it has become too expensive to repair them.

*The Second World War was a particularly hazardous time for the pier. Many in the south and east were regarded as potential landing stages for invading troops. Some, such as Bournemouth, Deal and Folkestone had whole sections blown out. On the west coast Minehead pier was destroyed to provide a clear line of sight for local gun batteries. Plymouth and Eastbourne piers were damaged by enemy action. In the picture below we see Deal Pier in 1940 suffering the fate of a damaged ship slicing right through it.*

## THE MORECAMBE DISASTER

In September 1895 the *Illustrated London News* reported on an accident that had taken place at Morcambe :

> Here on Monday September 9th at eleven in the morning, the landing stage at the end of the pleasure pier, which projects far into the sea, was crowded with people, waiting to get on board the steam-boat Empress, for an excursion to Blackpool. Part of the floor of this structure, composed of iron gratings, supported by iron piers too slender for the unusual weight of such a throng, suddenly broke down beneath them; about fifty men, women and children were thrown into the water. It was not deep enough, on all sides, to drown them immediately, and many of them clung to the undamaged parts of the landing stage, or to the pier,

until they could be relieved, there being no high waves. But the fall or shock had probably stunned a few of the weaker, and others had suffered contusions of the limbs, which made them unable to stand, while some endeavouring to reach the steam-boat, got into deep water. An elderly lady, Mrs. Ralph of Carlisle, was taken up drowned, and laid upon the deck of the steam-boat. Several other women, unconscious and almost lifeless when they were lifted out of the water, presently revived; but Clara Illingworth, wife of the caretaker of the Methley Board School, near Leeds, and a young man named Priestley, were drowned, their bodies not being recovered until low tide in the evening. Fractured legs and severe lacerations were suffered by three or four ladies, and there was one case of concussion of the spine, besides many injuries from the effects of the shock, or of the immersion, which might prove more or less serious. Yet the disaster might easily have caused a much greater loss of life.

What dangers might a pier be subject to? Why do you think piers have been so prone to disaster?

*Clevedon Pier in a state of collapse. On October 17 1970 Clevedon Pier was given a routine test for structural soundness in order to obtain insurance cover. Temporary water tanks were put up on the pier and it collapsed under the weight. Despite the efforts of a local preservation society, the pier remains derelict.*

# Seaside Fun and Entertainments

*Volk's electric railway in Brighton, 1890s. In this unique, monster-like contraption, people were "trundled" through the sea at high or low tide and presumably, as indicated in this advertisement, by day or by night.*
▽

There has always been lots to do at the seaside: goat carriages, donkey rides, brass bands, minstrel shows, Punch and Judy, sandcastles and amusement arcades, to name but a few. Some are quite new; others have not changed at all over the years, particularly those where you entertain yourselves.

Compare and contrast a weekday at the seaside with a Sunday. Is there any difference today between weekdays and a Sunday at the seaside?

*Donkey rides on the sands at Blackpool, c.1920. Does the age of the riders surprise you?* ▷

## SQUEALING, SQUALLING, SCREAMING...

Richard Jeffries in his essay, "The Open Air", gives a description of how people entertained themselves at the seaside in 1885:

> Mamma goes down to bathe with her daughters and the little ones; they take two machines at least; the pater comes to smoke his cigar; the young fellows of the family party come to look at "the women", as they irreverently speak of the sex.... Every seat is occupied; the boats and small yachts are filled; some of the children pour pebbles into the boats, some carefully throw them out; wooden spades are busy, sometimes they knock each other on the side of the head with them, sometimes they empty pails of sea water on a sister's frock. There is squealing, squalling, screaming, shouting, singing, bawling, howling, whistling, tin-trumpeting, and every luxury of noise. Two or three bands work away... a conjurer in red throws his heels in the air; several harps strum merrily different strains; fruit sellers push baskets into folk's faces; sellers of wretched needlework and singular baskets coated with shells thrust their rubbish into people's laps. These shell baskets date from George IV. The gingerbeer men and the newsboys cease not from troubling. Such a volume of uproar, such a complete organ of discord—I mean a whole organful—cannot be found anywhere else on the face of the earth in so comparatively small a space. It is a sort of triangular plot of beach crammed with everything that ordinarily annoys the ears and offends the sight.

How many sounds are mentioned here?

## SUNDAY BY THE SEA

At the beginning of this century people were very strict about Sundays. It was not much fun for children being at the seaside on "the Sabbath". In Bournemouth no trains were allowed until 1914, Sunday music was barred, and steamers were not allowed to call at the pier till 1929. In this extract from his *The Very First History of the English Seaside*, written in 1947, H.G. Stokes describes a Sunday by the sea at the turn of the century:

> In the strictest households blinds were drawn, silence reigned and complete inactivity prevailed. The adults meditated or frankly slept... but for children the seventh day was purgatory. Dolls and toys were locked away; even the Boys Own Paper was considered rather improper Sunday reading, and the sands were absolutely taboo, being reserved solely for the sea and for sinners.

# Pierrot Players and Punch and Judy

Punch and Judy and Pierrot players have been among the most popular seaside entertainment. Punch and Judy shows are still a regular feature on the beach. Pierrot players have not been seen for many years. They were most popular during the 1890s.

*By the mid-1890s Pierrot players had become a popular and common sight on the beaches. This photograph shows Pierrots at North Parade, Bridlington.*

## WATCHING THE PIERROTS

In an interview, Margaret Powell remembered her childhood days in Brighton at the beginning of the century. She was a poor girl, and she and her friends did not have much money. But they still managed to see the Pierrots:

And then there were the pierrot shows. Two in particular I remember; one was called the Quips and one was called the Follies. The Quips in particular. The men all came out dressed up in orange, black and silk baggy trousers and the girls in very short skirts and they used to come on with a song. It used to start with "We are the merry, merry Quips". And they used to come out with jokes. I suppose they were terrible jokes, but we children, we used to stand at the back, we thought they were marvellous. They used to fence it all round with seats, you used to pay either one and six or ninepence, but of course we never had anything like 1/6 or 9d, so we used to stand at the back, four of us, with one keeping an eye out, because every now and again one of the Quips would come round with a hat for the people who weren't paying for seats to put money in, so we used to shout out at the top of our voice. We had a password "four" that we used to shout out. We didn't know it had anything to do with golf; we used to shout out "four" and all four of us used to scuttle off like lightning. Because we never had any money and as soon as the coast was clear, back we came again, to watch again. And then of course there was the donkeys. Well there again we never had any money of course to go on the donkeys but nevertheless we used to be allowed to stand around them and stroke them and if we had anything in the way of bits of bread or carrots, or anything, we were allowed to feed them. Every year the same six donkeys came, or at any rate they looked the same to us. It was definitely the same man because he got older and older and older, and in the end he seemed to look like one of these donkeys. He got old and grey and shaggy. Anyway, you just couldn't help laughing.

Try to find out why the Pierrot players died out. Why do you think Punch and Judy shows have survived?

## THE PUNCH AND JUDY MAN

Here a proprietor of a Punch and Judy show describes his work. The extract, from an interview by Mayhew in the 1850s, shows how some of the people spoke:

I am the proprietor of a Punch's show.... I goes about with it myself, and performs inside the frame behind the green baize. I have a partner what plays the music — the pipes and drum; him as you see'd with me. I have been five-and-twenty years at the business.... I formerly was five months out of employment, knocking about, living first on my wages (*which he had earned as a servant*) and then on my clothes, till all was gone but the few rags on my back. So I began to think that the Punch-and-Judy business was better than starving after all...

The first person who went out with me was my wife. She used to stand outside and keep the boys from peeping through the baize, whilst I was performing behind it; and she used to collect the money afterwards as well. I carried the show and trumpet, and she the box...

Now I often show twenty times in the day, and get scarcely a bare living at it. We start on our rounds... in the morning and remain out till dark at night...

We in generally walks from twelve to twenty miles every day, and carries the show, which weighs a good half-hundred at the least... Wherever we goes we are sure of plenty of boys for a hindrance; but they've got no money, bother 'em. And they'll follow us for miles, so that we're often compelled to go miles to avoid them...

They'll throw one another's caps into the frame while I'm inside on it, and do what we will, we can't keep 'em from poking their fingers through the baize and having holes to peep through. Watering places is werry good in July and August. Punch mostly goes down to the seaside with the quality.

"The quality" meant the toffs (the well-to-do).

# Rescue at Sea

The sea has its beauties, but when the weather turns bad, it can be a dangerous place for holiday-makers, fishermen and sailors. Lifeboats and air/sea rescue services have saved the lives of many.

## WRECK ON THE GOODWINS

In early January 1881 the weather was dark, foggy and bitter along the east coast. The three-masted Indian Chief had just reached the mouth of the Thames after a long and difficult four days since leaving Middlesborough. With a crew of 28, she was on her way to Yokohama with general cargo.

Just after three in the morning disaster struck. The mate later described what happened:

Shortly after the Knock Light had hove in sight the wind shifted to the eastward and brought a squall of rain.... The Long Sand was to leeward, and finding that we were drifting that way the order was given to put the ship about. It was very dark, the wind breezing up sharper and sharper, and cold as death...

... there was much confusion, the vessel heeling over, and all of us knew the sands were close aboard. The ship paid off, but at the critical moment the spanker-boom sheet fouled the wheel. Still, we managed to get her round; but scarcely were the braces belayed and the ship on the starboard tack, when she struck ground broadside on. She was a softwood-built ship, and she trembled as though she would go to pieces at once, like a pack of cards.

Sheets and halliards were let go, but no man durst venture aloft. Every moment threatened to bring her spars crashing about us, and the thundering and beating of the canvas made the masts buckle and jump like fishing-rods.

We then kindled a great flare, and sent up rockets, and our signals were answered by the Sunk lightship and the Knock. We all cheered at that.

Meanwhile, the Ramsgate lifeboat was launched with Coxwain Charles Fish in command of a crew of eleven. The gale had become strong and the lifeboat had a long way to go, so a tug, the paddle-steamer *Vulcan*, was taken on to tow her. The lifeboatmen were soon soaked to the skin, but they were not able to find the wreck before dark and it was pounded by heavy seas all night, during which time some of the men on board were drowned. The lifeboat had to lie low and wait till dawn. When the wreck was found, eleven survivors were taken off. A reporter on the *Daily Telegraph* gave an eyewitness account of the landing of the lifeboat and tug:

> I recall the coming ashore of their crews; the lifeboatmen with their great cork-jackets around them, the tugmen in streaming oilskins, the faces of many of them livid with the cold, their eyes dim with the bitter vigil they had kept, and the furious blowing of the spray. And I remember the smile that here and there lighted up the weary faces as first one and then another caught sight of a wife or a sister in the crowd waiting to greet and accompany the brave hearts to the warmth of their humble homes.
>
> One by one the survivors came along the pier -- eleven alive but scarcely living men, most of them clad in oilskins and walking with bowed backs, drooping heads and nerveless arms. There was blood on the faces of some, circled with a white encrustation of salt, and this same salt filled the hollows of their eyes and streaked their hair with lines that looked like snow. . . . They were all saturated with brine; they were soaked with sea-water to the very marrow of the bones.

Describe the conditions that the crews had to face. In what state were the survivors when they landed?

*Launching the Peterhead life-boat, 1960s. Today, lifeboats, in conjunction with helicopters, provide an invaluable service. Lifeboatmen often sacrifice their lives to the cause of rescue at sea, as happened in the Penlee disaster in Cornwall, in 1981.*
▽

◁ *The wreck on the Goodwins, showing the tug* Vulcan.

# Rich and Poor Holidays

Where you went on holiday, for how long, and what sort of things you did when you got there, depended very much (and still does depend) on how rich or how poor a background you came from.

## ABSOLUTELY ALWAYS IN CORNWALL

Esther Stokes came from a wealthy London family. She was born in 1895. Here are some of her childhood memories of holidays:

Holidays were absolutely always in Cornwall. There was no alternative. Nowhere. When we lived in Streatham, Rickards, the famous bus people who still exist, used to send two small horse buses. And the family and the luggage all piled into these two buses. And the children in freshly starched pinafores were allowed to sit on the box with the coachman.

All the maids went with us and then the caretakers would move into the London house, a man and his wife. And another interesting thing about family life in those days, my mother always had an extra kitchen maid, a second kitchen maid, in the summer holidays just to prepare the vegetables, because the mere fact of beans and peas and potatoes and carrots for so many, it's a morning's work. And there weren't any potato peelers or any mixers or anything. It's all had to be done by hand. In the holidays we girls had a very nice sitting room with a piano in it and we were supposed to keep that tidy...

Father Corbishley was the parish priest of St Mawgan which was our parish in Cornwall and he was also the chaplain to the convent which was the Convent of the Carmelite nuns. And of course he was a friend of the family and often came to us, and we rather ragged the poor old man really. We used to play cards with him. We always said he cheated. I don't think he did really but we said he did. The boys had lots of friends to stay from Downside, they were at Downside School, and they used to bring friends home, particularly the young priests, who having taken the

*They don't look too happy but presumably they are pleased to have got away from the stress and toil of town-life. (1900s)*

vows of poverty never had much opportunity for holidays. And they used to come and stay and play tennis and bathe with us and go long expeditions. And of course having the chapel was a great advantage 'cause we had daily mass. My grandmother never stayed with us. She stayed in a hotel nearby. But during the holiday times some of the favourite uncles and aunts used to come to stay.

*A contrast in styles. This child from a wealthy background in the 1900s wears a well-cut suit and has well-made shoes on his feet.*

### SALFORD POOR CHILDREN'S CAMP

By contrast, when he was young, Mr Dodson went to the Salford Poor Children's Camp. Here are some of his recollections of it in the 1900s:

Oh you took nothing. You were lucky if you took 2d with you for the week to spend — you were rich. I mean so, although money meant something, it meant nothing really because nobody had money so you didn't envy. If somebody there had 4d, they were rich. Now you were issued with a — so that you would all look the same — you were all given a thick navy blue, like a seaman's jersey. You all got this. And in red on the navy blue across here, it had Salford Poor Children's Camp. So everybody knew where you were from. But you never went out of the camp on your own, you were always under escort. And I think — and you were under canvas, you all slept in tents, except the dining room was a wooden building and you lived mainly on beans. You had beans all the time.

We were a tough lot of kids, but there were restrictions. Remember we were used, we were brought up to authority, you know. Authority was respected. Mr. Harding, who was the superintendent, no doubt a smashing bloke, smart, he had to hold all this lot together. So he was very strict, seemed to be to us. And there's no such thing as writing home complaining cause the letters were censored.

What do you think were the similarities and differences between the two holidays described here?

39

# Holiday Camps

William Butlin organized the first holiday camp in 1936, on a site between Skegness and Mablethorpe. The idea was to provide, at a reasonable price, communal amusements and restaurants and a network of self-contained chalets within easy reach of the sea. Since then, millions have spent their holidays in a Butlin's camp — looked after by a "Redcoat", in a red blazer, who helps to organize the entertainments. Other camps, like Pontin's, have also been very popular.

## A DAY AT BUTLIN'S, 1946

This is what a day at Butlin's, Clacton-on-Sea, in 1946 would have provided:

9.30 a.m. Kiddies' Playtime in the Playroom (Parents' Free Hour).

9.45 a.m. Special Motor Coach trip to the Norfolk Broads, including a motor Launch trip on the Broads—Arrive back in Camp by 9.15 p.m.

10.00 a.m. You should be getting really fit by now! How about coming along and have some more Games and Exercises on

N.A.L.G.O. Holiday Camp  Cayton Bay Nr Scarborough

◁ Holiday camps have also been provided by trade unions. This postcard shows the view from the N.A.L.G.O. (National Association of Local Government Officers) Camp.

On holiday at Butlin's, Skegness in the 1930s. The buildings look like concrete barracks, but everyone seems to be having a good time. Look at the styles of the bathing costumes and compare them with those on pages 22-23.

the Sports Field.

10.30 a.m. Butlin Beginners' Swimming Class at the Pool. Two more days now to get that Certificate.

10.30 a.m. Uncle Mac will entertain children of all ages on the Playground.

10.45 a.m. Organized Amble. A pleasant walk along the Coast. Meet at the Pool.

11.00 a.m. Final rehearsal for Campers' Concert in the Kent Theatre. Your last chance to mount that ladder to the stars!

11.00 a.m. Special attraction!! Lads' and Lasses' Softball Match. The Campers of Kent *v.* Campers of Gloucester.

11.00 a.m. Boxing Instruction in the Gym. Some last-minute tips from Reggie Meen for to-night's contests.

11.00 a.m. In a few hours' time Harry Davidson and his Orchestra will be playing for you. Come along and learn the Fifth and Last Figure of the Lancers, with Arthur Wood at the Compton Organ.

11.15 a.m. Kiddies' Fun and Games on the Green (Under 7's).

11.45 a.m. Health and Beauty class, for 16's to 60's, on the Green.

2.30 p.m. Butlin's Grand Carnival! There will be a Grand Parade of Decorated Bicycles, Decorated Juvenile Bicycles — Adults', Junior Campers' and Kiddies' Fancy Dress Parade (Best Costume, Most Original and Most Humorous). Also Junior Campers' Inter-House Dancing Competition. The Parade will be headed by the Holiday Lovely of the week, the most charming Junior Camper and the Kiddies' Holiday Lovely, on the Sports Field. Alvin Gould and his Carnival Band will be there too. Followed by the world famous Frogmen at the Pool, and a Swimming Gala, at approx. 4.30 p.m. Events: 1 Length Free Style, 1 Length Breast Stroke; Diving Competition; 1 Length Backstroke; 6 x 1 Length Inter-House Relay; Veterans' 1 Length.

4.00 p.m. Toddlers' Tea Time, in the Noah's Ark.

4.30 p.m. Uncle Mac with Punch and Judy on the Playground.

8.00 p.m. Inter-House Novices' Boxing Competition in the Gym. And an exhibition bout: Reggie Meen, Heavyweight Champion of Great Britain, 1931 and 1932; and Ray Salmon, Army Heavyweight Champion, Western Command.

8.30 p.m. Campers' Concert in the Theatre.

9.00 p.m. Special attraction! Old Fashioned dancing to Harry Davidson and his Orchestra.

10.15 p.m. Arthur Wood on the Compton Organ will take over until 10.45 p.m.

10.25 p.m. Penny on the Drum.

10.45 p.m. Old Fashioned Dancing Again with Harry Davidson and his Orchestra.

11.00 p.m. A Demonstration of the Lancers will be given by members of the Entertainment Staff.

11.45 p.m. Good night Campers.

What sort of people would go to a holiday camp? From your own experience or by talking to someone else who has been to one, find out whether a typical day at a holiday camp nowadays is any different from in 1946.

# Seaside Postcards

Some of the earliest postcards did not give a favourable or sympathetic view of working people. They were much in the style of the picture on page 12, "Waiting for the excursion train in 1880". Around 1914 comic and cheeky postcards became more popular — and have remained so to this day. With more people going to the sea, more wanted to write to those left behind and different styles of postcards were produced in their millions — some idyllic scenes, some comic, some very detailed, some in colour . . .

*A sea trip in 1934.* ▷

**We've been watching the 'all-in' wrestling here!**

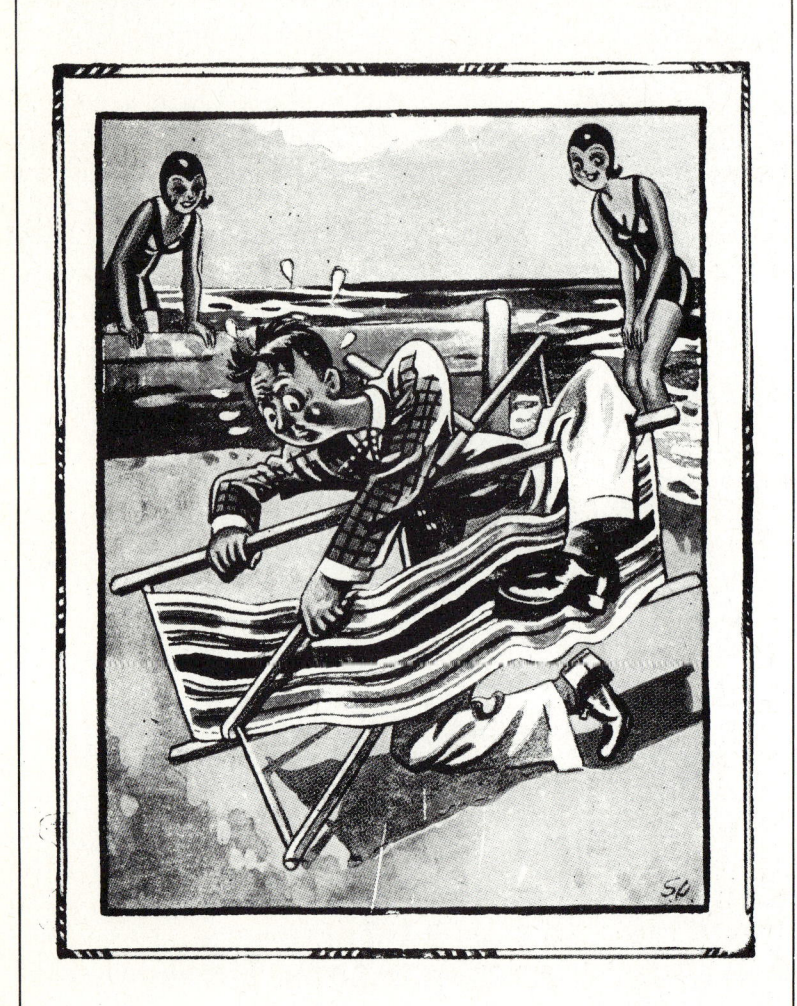

◁ *A comic postcard from the 1920s — and not as "rude" as some you might have seen at the seaside.*

*Five scenes from Angmering, Sussex, 1950s.* ▷

Why do postcards sell in their millions? Collect as many seaside postcards as you can — and, together with the ones printed here, see how many types of postcard you can find.

L9B

Shopping Centre
Palm Court Hotel
South Strand
ANGMERING-ON-SEA
Sands

# Holidays Today

Most of us have been to the seaside — for a day, a week or longer. We descend on the seaside, in greater numbers than ever, often putting a strain on the facilities and the natural beauty of the coastline. As the seaside towns fill up, many people have taken to tents, caravans and caravanettes, which tend to cover whole stretches of coastline — though quiet spots can always be found.

Increasingly also, people have been going abroad for their holidays — with the Spanish and Italian coasts amongst the most popular places. Charter flights and group holidays have reduced the cost of holidays abroad, which are now within the reach of many more people.

## A WEEK IN CORNWALL, 1982

Rose Baker is an office cleaner who lives in Bristol. Here she recalls a recent holiday (1982) in Newquay, Cornwall:

> We went to Newquay just for a week. We go because we like it there. We go there every year. The sea is nice and the people are nice who we stay with. We stay in the Pentrevah Hotel. About 21 bedrooms — a family concern. The landlady is very nice. It's bed and breakfast, and evening meal.
>
> They have two little shows on a Thursday and Tuesday. They've got a little dance floor that you can dance on — they've got a television room where you can watch television if you want to. The meals are excellent.
>
> I've been going for eight or nine years now, and I never get bored. Four of us go, me, my husband, my brother and his wife. We go by car. We meet the same people every year, or nearly all the same people. They come from all over the place — Doncaster, Wales, London.

## IBIZA, ON A PACKAGE HOLIDAY

Sadie and Phil Westbury have been going on a package holiday abroad for the last thirty years. This year (1982) they went to San Antonio, the capital of Ibiza.

> We always choose a package because it gives an opportunity to browse through brochures where full details are always available. We choose an overseas seaside resort mainly because of guaranteed good weather and have never yet had a holiday spoilt through bad weather.
>
> The hotels are fully illustrated in the brochures so we can see what we are getting within our price range. We arrange the holiday through a travel agent whose representative is always available at the resort. We usually select Majorca, the Spanish mainland or Italy. This year we chose Ibiza — one of the other popular Balearic Islands — having stayed there many years ago. Our hotel was in San Antonio. We went in June because it is cooler, even though the temperature is in the eighties — August is very much hotter. We book for two weeks. The fare is the
>
> The seaside is clean. There you've got the lot and you can please yourselves. There's the headlands, we have a walk round the beaches, cups of tea, sitting up on the green watching the bowling and looking down over the sea, reading the paper, reading me book . . .

same as for one week's holiday — but the overall cost is better value for two weeks. This year we paid £249 per person, which includes full board, flight and gratuities. A holiday for us should include being able to relax around a swimming pool, visiting local places of interest, i.e. half day excursions and evening entertainment at the hotel, or within easy reach. We like to be near to the shopping area and our hotel always has a sea view. We had a good choice of food at the hotel, and now that most Spanish hotels have changed over to self-service it is ideal for our needs.

We have met visitors from Spain, the Netherlands and Germany and of course the UK. Language is no barrier as everyone speaks English.

For our next holiday we hope to go to a hotel on the Spanish mainland.

Para-sailing, Negril, Jamaica. The most modern trend is perhaps for adventure sports and activity holidays, often in countries further away than Europe. Compare this sort of holiday with the first trips to the seaside described on pages 6-15. What reasons are there for the changes?

Make a survey of your family and friends. Compile six brief accounts of their holidays and compare them.

The holidays described here went smoothly. Can you describe a holiday where things went wrong?

## Difficult Words

| | |
|---|---|
| bathing machine | small wooden hut on wheels, to take bathers to the sea. |
| belayed | secure. |
| charabanc | motorised or horse-drawn coach, with many seats. |
| commensurate | measured by a similar standard. |
| contiguous | near to. |
| contusion | bruise. |
| desecration | violation of the sanctity. |
| dipper | someone who helped other people bathe. |
| dissertation | exposition or piece of writing on a particular subject. |
| halliard | rope, tackle for raising or lowering sail. |
| laceration | tear in flesh. |
| mal de mer | sea sickness. |
| omniscient | all-knowing. |
| pharynx | cavity behind the mouth and nose. |
| promenade | to walk; or a place to walk along the sea-front. |
| putrefaction | process of rotting away. |
| redcoat | a guide in Butlin's holiday camp. |
| sheets | ropes or chains at lower corner of sail. |
| spanker-boom | sail. |
| submarine | under the sea. |

### CONVERSION TABLE

| NEW MONEY | | OLD MONEY |
|---|---|---|
| 1p | = | 2.4d |
| 5p | = | 1s. (1 shilling) |
| 50p | = | 10s. (10 shillings) |
| £1 | = | £1 |
| | | 12d = 1 shilling |
| | | 20 shillings = £1 |

## Biographical Notes

BAKER, Rose  A Bristol office cleaner in her 60s.

BASHFORTH, Hedley  A teacher born in the 1950s.

CHAPLIN, Charlie  (1889-1927) Famous film comedian of the early cinema.

GUNN, Martha  An eighteenth-century "dipper" at Brighton.

HUMPHRIES, Jim  Born in 1921 in Stoke on Trent, the son of a miner. He works in the insurance business.

HUMPHRIES, Marjorie  Born in Exeter in 1924. Her father was a printer. She was brought up in Filton, Bristol. She has worked as a telephonist.

JEFFRIES, Richard  Born in 1848 in Wiltshire, he wrote about the countryside and its people as well as novels and other essays. He died of tuberculosis in 1887.

KILVERT, Reverend Francis  A clergyman who kept a vivid diary during the 1870s. Born in 1840, he died aged 40.

LEE, Laurie  Poet and writer born in Gloucestershire. Worked for Ministry of Information during Second World War. His best-selling autobiography, *Cider with Rosie* (1959) was followed with *As I Walked Out One Midsummer Morning* (1969).

MAYHEW, Henry  A nineteenth-century social investigator. He interviewed hundreds of "ordinary" people, with a view to finding out about their living conditions.

MILTON, Bertha  Born at the end of the nineteenth century, she comes from Barton Hill in Bristol.

POWELL, Margaret  A domestic servant, she has become famous for writing about her experiences, particularly *Below Stairs*.

RUSSEL, Richard  A fashionable London "quack" in the eighteenth century — some called him a physician.

SMOLLETT, Tobias George (1721-71) Born in Dumbartonshire of good family. Surgeon, journalist and novelist. His books are now largely forgotten.

STOKES, Esther Born in 1895 of wealthy parents. Her father was a barrister and her mother from a manufacturing family. In later years she was President of the Women's Institute.

WESTBURY, Phil Semi-retired, he works part-time in a store, in the school uniforms department.

WESTBURY, Sadie A secretary to an insurance broker in London.

## Map

A map of British seaside resorts which once had piers. Those with the anme underlined have a pier still existing.

# Index

Bank Holidays 12
bathing machines 6, 7, 9, 20
Bedminster Ebenezer Sisterhood 15
Blackpool 8, 10
boarding houses 16
Bognor 12
Bournemouth Pier 28, 30
Bridlington 8
Brighton (Brighthelmstone) 3, 6, 8, 15, 18, 32, 34, 35
Broadstairs 23
Burney, Fanny 8
Butlin's 40, 41

caravans 16, 17
chalets 16, 17, 26
Chaplin, Charlie 26
charabancs 15
Clacton 40, 41
Clevedon Pier 30, 31
Cornwall 38, 44

day excursions 10, 11, 12
Deal Pier 30
dipper 8, 20
donkeys 34, 35

Eastbourne 10
Exmouth 26, 27

George III 3, 8
George IV 3
guest house 18
Gunn, Martha 20

Hardy, Thomas 24
Hastings 10, 29
holiday camps 4, 14, 40, 41
holidays, official 10
holidays, unofficial 10
holidays, paid 12, 14
holidays, week-long 3
Humberstone 17
Humphries, Marjorie 26, 27
Hunstanton 14

Ibiza 44, 45
Industrial Revolution 3, 10
Isle of Wight 22

Jeffries, Richard 33

Kilvert, Francis 22

Lee, Laurie 25

Mablethorpe 16, 17
Margate, 8, 10, 21
Morecambe Pier, accident 30, 31

N.A.L.G.O. holiday camp 40
nude bathing 20, 21, 22, 23

Osborne, Professor 29

Packman, Arthur 19
parasols 3
Parker, Florence 18
Pierrot Players 34, 35

piers 28, 29, 30, 31
postcards 42, 43
Powell, Margaret 34, 35
Punch and Judy 14, 34, 35

railways 10, 11, 12, 14
Ramsgate 21
road transport 12, 14
Russel, Richard 6, 7

Sabbath, desecration of 11
Salford Poor Children's Camp 39
Sandgate 19
Scarborough 6, 7
sea, dangers of 24
seawater 6, 7
Smollett, Tobias 20
Southend 10, 26
Southport 16, 28
Stokes, Esther 38
sunbathing 3
swimming costumes 20, 21, 22, 23

tents 16
transport, improvements 8
Trustthorpe 17

Volk's Electric Railway 32

Westbury, Phil and Sadie 44, 45
Weston-Super-Mare 22, 25
Weymouth 8
Wittie, Dr 6
Worthing 10
wreck on the Goodwins 36, 37